NOTT

Compiled by Julia Skinner

THE FRANCIS FRITH COLLECTION

www.francisfrith.com

First published in the United Kingdom in 2012 by The Francis Frith Collection®

This edition published exclusively for Identity Books in 2012 ISBN 978-1-84589-675-1

Text and Design copyright The Francis Frith Collection®
Photographs copyright The Francis Frith Collection® except where indicated.

British Library Cataloguing in Publication Data

Flavours of ... Nottinghamshire - Recipes
Compiled by Julia Skinner

The Francis Frith Collection
Oakley Business Park,
Wylye Road, Dinton,
Wiltshire SP3 5EU
Tel: +44 (0) 1722 716 376
Email: info@francisfrith.co.uk
www.francisfrith.com

Printed and bound in Malaysia
Contains material sourced from responsibly managed forests

Front Cover: **NEWARK-ON-TRENT, SHOPS IN STODMAN STREET 1906** 56494xp
Frontispiece: **NOTTINGHAM, THE QUEEN VICTORIA STATUE, MARKET SQUARE 1906** 56462
Contents: **SUTTON-ON-TRENT, CYCLISTS BY THE WESLEYAN CHAPEL 1909** 61817x

The colour-tinting is for illustrative purposes only, and is not intended to be historically accurate

CONTENTS

2   Soups

8   Cheese and Vegetable Dishes

16 Meat, Game and Poultry

36 Puddings, Pies and Desserts

48 Teatime and Baking

54 Francis Frith - Pioneer Victorian
    Photographer

RECIPE

LEEK AND POTATO SOUP

Much of the fertile land of Nottinghamshire is used for arable farming and vegetable production, with carrots, leeks and potatoes being especially important crops in the county's agricultural economy. Why not serve this soup with some Stilton and Walnut Scones – see recipe on page 53.

> 50g/2oz butter
> 2 leeks, trimmed, washed and chopped
> 1 small onion, finely chopped
> 350g/12oz potatoes
> 900ml/1½ pints chicken or vegetable stock
> Salt and pepper

Heat 25g/1oz of the butter in a large saucepan, add the leeks and onion and cook gently for 8-10 minutes, stirring occasionally to prevent sticking, until the vegetables are softened but not browned. Add the potatoes to the pan and cook, stirring occasionally, for a further 3-5 minutes, then add the stock and bring to the boil. Cover the pan and reduce the heat, then simmer gently for 30-40 minutes until the vegetables are very tender. Season to taste. Remove the pan from the heat and stir in the remaining butter, then serve the soup whilst it is still piping hot, with good crusty bread.

This can be sieved or liquidized if a smoother soup is preferred, then served with a swirl of cream and some freshly chopped parsley to finish.

NOTTINGHAMSHIRE'S MONSTER SPUD!

Nottinghamshire is a major potato-growing area of England, and in 2010 a Nottinghamshire gardener beat the world record for growing the largest potato ever recorded. In September 2010 the Guinness Book of Records officially recognised the monster spud grown in his back garden by Peter Glazebrook of Halam, near Newark, as the heaviest potato every grown – at a weight of 8 lbs 4oz (3.8kg), Mr Glazebrook made mashed potato of the previous world record of 7 lbs 13oz (3.5kg), which had stood since 1994.

NEWARK-ON-TRENT, SHOPS IN STODMAN STREET 56494x

BALDERTON, THE VILLAGE 1909 61813

RECIPE

CARROT AND GINGER SOUP

Nottinghamshire is one of the country's main carrot growing areas. New season carrot seed is sown in winter and early spring and the crop is then harvested from June to August, usually at night to protect the young, tender carrots from the heat of the sun; the harvesting of main crop carrots then takes place across the county until the first frosts of autumn. This soup is very quick and easy to prepare, and is a glorious golden-orange colour. The flavour of ginger is very subtle, but gives the soup a wonderful flavour and just a hint of spicy warmth, perfect for a winter's day.

> 675g/1½ lbs carrots
> 1 medium sized onion
> A small piece of fresh root ginger, peeled and cut about 2.5cm
>   (1 inch) square
> 50g/2oz butter
> 1.2 litres (2 pints) vegetable or chicken stock
> Salt and freshly ground black pepper
> 4-6 tablespoonfuls single or double cream, or natural yogurt,
>   to serve (optional)
> Fresh coriander leaves, finely chopped, to garnish (optional)

Scrub and trim the carrots and chop them into rounds. Peel and roughly chop the onion. Melt the butter in a large thick-bottomed pan and add the carrots and onion. Sweat the vegetables gently over a medium heat for 5 minutes. Grate the root ginger into the pan, stir it in and cook for a further 3 minutes. Add the stock, bring to the boil and simmer, covered, for 15 minutes.

Leave to cool slightly, then zap the soup in a blender or liquidizer until smooth. Return to the pan, season to taste and reheat. Put the soup into individual bowls and serve. It is fine to serve just as it is, but to make it extra special you can dress it up before serving with a garnish of chopped fresh coriander and a swirl of cream or natural yogurt.

STILTON CHEESE

Stilton, a creamy blue-veined cheese with an excellent flavour and a texture that softens as it blues and mellows, has become known as 'The King of Cheeses'. A 16 lb Stilton cheese takes 17 gallons of milk to produce, and at least two months to mature. It was first developed in the villages of east Leicestershire and Rutland, and became famous in the early 18th century when Mrs Frances Pawlett, a dairywoman who lived near Melton Mowbray, entered into a business arrangement with her brother-in-law Cooper Thornhill, who agreed to market her cheese. Mr Thornhill was the owner of the Bell Inn at Stilton (then in Huntingdonshire but now in Cambridgeshire). He began to introduce the cheese to travellers staying at the inn and it soon became very popular. So it was that the cheese was named after the town where it was sold and distributed from, rather than the place where it was made – it has never actually been made in Stilton.

By the early 20th century the making of Stilton cheese had extended to the neighbouring areas of Nottinghamshire and Derbyshire. The Stilton cheese-makers then sought legal protection for their product to prevent the development of inferior imitation cheese. Stilton is now one of the few cheeses granted a 'protected designation of origin' status by the European Commission, which in 1969 ruled that 'Stilton is a blue or white cheese made from full cream milk, with no applied pressure, forming its own crust or coat and made in cylindrical form, the milk coming from English dairy herds in the district of Melton Mowbray and the surrounding areas falling within the counties of Leicestershire (now including Rutland), Derbyshire and Nottinghamshire'. This means that there are strict codes for the quality of the cheese, and it can only be made in the designated counties. Only 6 dairies in the designated area are currently licensed to produce Stilton cheese, two of which are in Nottinghamshire: the Colston Bassett Dairy and Cropwell Bishop Creamery, both near Nottingham.

RECIPE

STILTON AND CELERY SOUP

This soup uses Stilton cheese, which is made in Nottinghamshire, but also includes Stilton's classic accompaniment of celery, which also has a place in the county's food history. Newdigate House on Castle Gate in Nottingham, an elegant 17th-century town house now used as offices, was where the Duc de Tallard, Marshall of France, spent a number of years in comfortable captivity after his forces were defeated by the Duke of Marlborough at the Battle of Blenheim in 1704, during the War of the Spanish Succession, and he was taken prisoner. His incarceration does not appear to have been too unpleasant, for he was allowed to bring his own retinue with him, including his own cooks, and he settled down to make the best of his time in captivity. Marshall Tallard was a keen gardener, and he is credited for introducing celery into English cuisine, which he cultivated in the garden of Newdigate House into the palatable form that we know today from the wild celery (Apium Graveolens) that he found growing wild in the area.

40g/1½ oz butter
1 onion, finely chopped
1 potato, cut into small cubes
1 whole head of celery, thinly sliced
900ml/1½ pints chicken or vegetable stock
115g/4oz Stilton cheese, crumbled
150ml/ ¼ pint single cream
Salt and freshly ground black pepper

Melt the butter in a large pan. Add the onion and cook over a medium heat for 5 minutes until it is transparent. Add the potato and celery and cook for a further 5 minutes until the vegetables begin to soften and brown. Add the stock, bring to the boil, then reduce heat, cover the pan and simmer for 30-40 minutes, until the vegetables are very soft. Allow it to cool for a few minutes, then liquidize the soup in a blender, return it to the pan and season to taste. Heat the soup through to just below the boil, then remove the pan from the heat, add the cheese and stir until it has melted. Stir in the cream and reheat just before serving, being careful not to allow the soup to boil.

RECIPE

BLUE SHROPSHIRE CHEESE AND WATERCRESS FLAN

As well as Stilton, another tasty blue cheese made in Nottinghamshire nowadays is Blue Shropshire, also known as Shropshire Blue. This is softer and creamier than Stilton, with a sharp, strong flavour, and is coloured orange with annatto, a natural food colouring. It was first made in the 1970s in Scotland by a cheese-maker who had trained in the making of Stilton cheese in Nottinghamshire. It was called Shropshire Blue as a marketing ploy, and is now made by the Cropwell Bishop and Colston Bassett dairies in Nottinghamshire, alongside their excellent Stilton cheeses.

This recipe makes a delicious savoury flan flavoured with Blue Shropshire cheese and the fresh, tangy taste of watercress. It is ideal served either warm or cold for summer lunches with a salad, or taken on a picnic to eat cold. You can use Stilton cheese in this recipe instead if you want to, but the delicious Blue Shropshire cheese is well worth trying if you have not discovered it yet.

175g/6oz plain flour
75g/3oz butter or margarine
A pinch of salt
Freshly ground black pepper
150g/5oz Blue Shropshire cheese,
    de-rinded and cut into thin slices
3 eggs, beaten
300ml/ ½ pint fresh milk
1 medium onion, peeled and finely chopped
75g/3oz fresh watercress (trimmed weight),
    with the thick stalks trimmed off

Pre-heat the oven to 200°F/400°F/Gas Mark 6, and place a baking tray in the oven to heat up. Grease a flan tin or quiche dish 20-24cms (8-9 inches) in diameter.

Put the flour into a mixing bowl with a pinch of salt, and rub the butter or margarine into the flour until the mixture resembles fine breadcrumbs. Mix in 2-3 tablespoonfuls of cold water, just enough to form the mixture into a firm dough, then knead the dough lightly until it is smooth and elastic. Roll out the dough on a lightly floured surface, and use it to line the greased flan tin or dish.

Place a piece of greaseproof paper with some baking beans on the pastry base, place the tin on the pre-heated baking tray in the oven (this helps the pastry base to cook through) and 'bake blind' for 10 minutes. Remove from the oven, take out the paper and baking beans and return to the oven for a further 5 minutes, to dry out the pastry base. Reduce the oven temperature to 190°C/375°F/Gas Mark 5.

Place the slices of cheese (and any crumbs) over the pastry base. Mix together the beaten eggs, the milk and the chopped onion, and season to taste with freshly ground black pepper but only a little salt, if needed, as the cheese will already contain some salt. Roughly chop the trimmed watercress and stir it into the egg mixture, combine it all together well, then pour the mixture into the pastry case.

Bake in the oven at the reduced temperature for 40-45 minutes, until the flan is cooked but not dry, and the filling is risen and firm to the touch.

This should not be eaten hot, straight from the oven, but leave the flan to cool a little and eat it warm, or otherwise eat it cold.

RECIPE

LEEK AND POTATO BAKE WITH BRAMLEY APPLE AND BUTTERNUT SQUASH

This recipe not only uses leeks and potatoes, vegetables that Nottinghamshire is famous for, but also the magnificent Bramley apple, which originated at Southwell in the county – see page 43. This bake can be eaten either as a filling main course that is full of flavour, or as a vegetable side dish. The topping of Red Leicester cheese gives the bake a lovely russet colour to match the orange butternut squash at its base, but you can use all Cheddar cheese if you prefer.

> 3 tablespoonfuls olive oil or sunflower oil
>
> 2 medium leeks, trimmed of roots and dark green outer leaves and cut into thin slices
>
> 2 garlic cloves, peeled and crushed, or finely chopped
>
> Salt and freshly ground black pepper
>
> 125ml/4½ fl oz good quality apple cider
>
> 1 tablespoonful roughly chopped fresh sage leaves
>
> 450g/1 lb butternut squash, peeled, seeded and cut into slices about 1cm (½ inch) thick
>
> 450g/1 lb Bramley cooking apples, peeled, cored and cut into slices
>
> 115g/4oz Cheddar cheese, grated
>
> 450g/1 lb potatoes, peeled and cut into thin slices
>
> 50g/2oz Red Leicester cheese, grated, for the topping (or the same amount of extra Cheddar, if preferred)

Pre-heat the oven to 180°C/350°F/Gas Mark 4.

Heat 2 tablespoonfuls of the oil in a large skillet or frying pan over a medium heat, add the sliced leeks, the garlic, and 2 tablespoonfuls of water, and season with salt and pepper. Cook, stirring occasionally, for 10 minutes, until the leeks are well softened. Add the cider, chopped sage leaves and the apple pieces and continue to cook for a further 5 minutes, then remove from the heat and put to one side.

Grease a large ovenproof dish. Arrange the slices of butternut squash in a layer on the bottom of the dish, and season lightly with salt and pepper. Spread the leek and apple mixture and its liquid evenly over the squash. Cover with a layer of 115g (4oz) of grated Cheddar cheese. Cover it all with an overlapping final layer of the potato slices. Brush the potato slices with the remaining tablespoonful of oil.

Cover the dish with its lid or with a tightly-fitted piece of kitchen foil, and bake in the pre-heated oven for about 1½ hours – test by pricking through the bake with a sharp knife, and return to the oven for about another half an hour if the potatoes and squash are not completely tender and cooked through.

When the bake is cooked, turn up the oven temperature to 225°C/450°F/Gas Mark. 8 Uncover the dish and sprinkle the remaining 50g/2oz of grated cheese (either Cheddar or Red Leicester) on top, then return to the hotter oven for about 10 minutes, until the cheese topping is melted and bubbling.

Remove the dish from the oven and allow the bake to rest for 10 minutes before serving.

RECIPE

NOTTINGHAMSHIRE BLEWITS

A wild mushroom which is common throughout Nottinghamshire, and a great favourite of local people, is the Wood Blewit (Lepista Nuda – also recognised as Clitocybe nuda). Wood Blewits are known by a number of names because of the lilac-blue tinge they have when young – 'blue buttons', 'blue stalks', 'blue tails', 'blewets' and 'blueys' – although they go a buff colour later, as they age. Wild picked Wood Blewits are available for sale during the growing season from September through to December, or perhaps January during a mild winter, but they are also commercially farmed nowadays and are often found in Nottinghamshire markets or greengrocers' shops, along with their close cousin, the Field Blewit (Lepista Saeva, or Clitocybe saeva), which are also popular.

Whenever collecting wild mushrooms and fungi yourself, be very careful about correctly identifying what you pick, as a mistaken identification can be very dangerous, even fatal. Take a good book with clear instructions to help you correctly identify the fungi, or, even better, go with an expert to help you find them. Wild mushrooms and fungi should always be collected into a basket, never a plastic bag, as this makes them deteriorate very quickly after being picked.

Blewits should never be consumed raw, as they can cause an allergic reaction or an unpleasant bout of indigestion in some people.

Blewits have an intense, distinctive spicy flavour. A traditional way of cooking them in Nottinghamshire is to stew them gently in milk and then thicken the liquid to make a sauce to serve them in, accompanied with mashed potato, as in this recipe. It can also be made with ordinary mushrooms if you can't get Blewits. This makes enough for 4 people.

450g/1 lb Field or Wood Blewits
25g/1oz butter for frying the Blewits
25g/1oz butter for making the sauce
550ml/1 pint milk
25g/1oz plain flour (about 3 level tablespoonfuls)
1 large onion
Salt and freshly ground black pepper
Enough potatoes for 4 people, and butter and milk or
    cream to mash them with

Remove the stems from the mushrooms and cut them into pieces.
Peel the onion and roughly chop it. Melt 25g (1oz) of butter in a large
heavy-bottomed pan and gently fry the chopped onion and mushroom
stalks for about 5 minutes until they are soft. Cut the mushrooms into
mouth-sized chunks and add to the pan, then add the milk. Bring the
mixture to a gentle boil, then reduce the heat to very low and simmer
gently for about 45 minutes, topping up the pan with a little more milk
if necessary. During this time, peel the potatoes, put them in a pan of
salted water, cover and bring to the boil, then turn down to a simmer
and cook for 20-30 minutes until the potatoes are tender.

When the mushrooms are cooked, remove from the heat, drain and put
to one side, reserving the liquid. Melt the remaining 25g (1oz) of butter
in the pan and stir in the flour, mixing it all together well. Cook on a low
heat for 2-3 minutes, stirring, then gradually blend in the mushroom
cooking liquid, adding a little at a time and stirring constantly as it
thickens, to make a roux sauce. Bring the sauce to the boil, then reduce
the heat to low, add the mushrooms and season the sauce to taste with
a little salt and freshly ground black pepper. Let the mixture simmer for
5 minutes, stirring occasionally to make sure it does not stick and burn.
Drain the cooked potatoes and mash them with a little butter and milk
or cream. Serve with a heap of mashed potato on a plate with a well in
the centre, filled with the mushroom mixture.

RECIPE

OVEN-BAKED CARROTS WITH HONEY AND MUSTARD

Nottinghamshire is one of Britain's main carrot producing areas – see page 5. This is an unusual and delicious way of cooking carrots to serve as a vegetable accompaniment, which gives them a wonderful flavour.

> 450g/1 lb carrots
> 2 tablespoonfuls water
> 2 tablespoonfuls sunflower oil
> 2 tablespoonfuls runny honey
> 1 tablespoonful wholegrain mustard
> Salt and freshly ground black pepper

Pre-heat the oven to 190°C/375°F/Gas Mark 5. Scrub the carrots and trim off the ends, then chop them into chunky sticks.

Put the carrot pieces into a shallow ovenproof dish. In a bowl, mix together the water, oil, honey and mustard, and season to taste with a little salt and freshly ground black pepper. Pour the mixture over the carrots in the oven dish, and stir until the carrots have all been coated with the mixture.

Cover the dish with its lid, or a piece of close-fitting kitchen foil, and bake in the pre-heated oven for 50-60 minutes, until the carrots are tender.

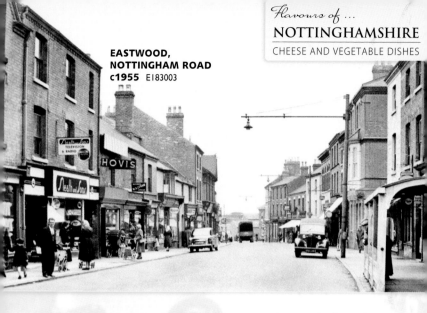

**EASTWOOD,
NOTTINGHAM ROAD
c1955** E183003

Nottinghamshire assumed much of its present character in the 18th century, when Enclosure Acts divided up the old medieval open fields of the county's villages into hawthorn-hedged small fields, and mechanised industry began to arrive in its towns and cities. In the 19th century, cotton mills and machine-lace factories eventually supplanted the hand looms, stocking-frames and lace bobbins of cottage industries where hosiery and lace were made by home-workers, and deep coal-mining transformed other parts of the county. Some of the photographs in this book show Nottinghamshire in the 1950s and 1960s, when coal mines still functioned all along the west of the county, supplying the huge coal-fired power stations along the River Trent by barge and railway. One of the biggest changes for Nottinghamshire within living memory was the closure in the 1980s of virtually all its coal mines, following the conversion of the River Trent power stations to gas. A famous son of a Nottinghamshire coal miner was the author D H Lawrence, who was born at No 8a Victoria Street in Eastwood in 1885 – his father worked at the Brinsley Pit near the town. The house is now a museum to D H Lawrence, converted back to how it would have looked when he lived there as a child.

15

RECIPE

FAGGOTS WITH ONION AND RED WINE GRAVY

In both rural areas and the industrial towns and cities of the Midlands in the past, where money was often short, people had to make the best possible use of economical cuts of meat, and many dishes evolved using offal, off-cuts and cheap parts of the animal. These traditional dishes included cow heel jelly, pigs' trotters, chitterlings, tripe and onions (see page 18), haslet (a meat loaf that is eaten cold, cut into slices) and faggots, which were often called 'Poor Man's Goose' in many parts of England in the past. Home-made faggots are very nutritious, and this recipe brings the dish up to date with a special gravy. If mincing up all the meat yourself does not appeal, ask your butcher to do it for you.

For the faggots:
25g/1oz unsalted butter
1 medium onion, peeled and finely chopped
175g/6oz minced pigs' liver
2 lambs' or pigs' hearts, trimmed and cut into chunks
450g/1 lb belly pork, trimmed and rind removed
Half a teaspoonful of ground mace
4 tablespoonfuls freshly chopped chives
1 teaspoonful freshly chopped sage
1 egg, beaten
Salt and freshly ground pepper
115g/4oz fresh white breadcrumbs
25g/1oz beef dripping or 3 tablespoonfuls olive oil

For the gravy:
4 red onions, peeled, and with each onion cut into 8 wedges
4 sprigs of fresh thyme
1 tablespoonful olive oil
900ml/1½ pints fresh beef stock
300ml/ ½ pint red wine
Salt and freshly ground black pepper

Melt the butter in a small saucepan and add the onion. Cook until soft and transparent, then leave to cool slightly.

Place the belly pork onto a chopping board and cut into portions. Place the minced pigs' liver into a large glass bowl and place under the blade of a mincer. Using a fine blade of the mincer, mince the pork belly and lambs' or pigs' heart directly into the bowl with the pigs' liver. Add the cooled chopped onions, mace, chives, sage, beaten egg and salt and pepper. Stir in the breadcrumbs. Using your hands, shape the mixture into 12 patties. Place them on a plate and chill in the fridge for about 1 hour.

Pre-heat the oven to 200°C/400°F/Gas Mark 6. Place the onion wedges into a large roasting pan or ovenproof dish. Add the thyme and drizzle over the olive oil. Place in the pre-heated oven and roast uncovered for 40 minutes until the onions are caramelised.

Meanwhile heat the dripping or olive oil in a large frying pan. Fry the faggots until golden brown on both sides.
Place the stock and wine in a small saucepan, bring to the boil and reduce by a third. Remove the roasted onions from the oven and lay the faggots on top. Pour over the gravy liqueur. Reduce the oven temperature to 180°C/350°F/Gas Mark 4 and cook the faggots for 40 minutes.

Place two to three faggots onto a plate. Top with a spoonful of the onions and pour over the gravy.

Serve the faggots with mashed potatoes and green vegetables – peas are the traditional accompaniment to faggots.

RECIPE

TRIPE AND ONIONS

Another dish that was very popular all over the Midlands in the past was tripe and onions. Many people nowadays are averse to the thought of eating tripe, but for those who like it, it is a very good dish, succulent in texture. Tripe is the edible stomach linings of an ox or cow. The first lining is called 'blanket', the second 'honeycomb' and the third 'double' or 'thick seam'. The appearance of the three linings is different, but they all taste the same. There are a number of traditional methods of preparing tripe, but one of the favourite methods is given here, plain and simple, with the tripe slow-cooked with onions for several hours, simmered in milk which is then used to make a rich creamy sauce to accompany it. Tripe is not often found in supermarkets, so you will probably need to get it from a traditional butcher, if you are lucky enough to still have one locally. Ask for a mixture of all the different parts of tripe for this dish. This amount is enough for 4 people.

> 450g/1 lb best prepared and dressed tripe, washed
> 3 large onions, peeled and sliced
> 550ml/1 pint milk
> 25g/1oz butter
> 25g/1oz plain flour
> 1 bay leaf
> A pinch of freshly grated nutmeg
> 1 level teaspoonful of dry mustard powder
> Salt and freshly ground black pepper
> 1 rounded tablespoonful of finely chopped fresh parsley

Place the tripe in a saucepan and cover with lightly salted cold water. Bring to the boil, then remove from the heat, drain the tripe and rinse it under cold running water. Cut the tripe into 2.5cm (1 inch) pieces.

Put a layer of the onions in the rinsed-out pan, then the tripe, then the rest of the onions. Pour in the milk, and add the bay leaf, the freshly grated nutmeg and a pinch of salt. Put the pan on a medium heat and bring the milk very slowly to just below the boil, then reduce the heat to very low, cover the pan with its lid and leave to simmer gently for as long as possible, until the tripe is very tender – at least 2 hours, longer if you can. Stir occasionally to prevent any sticking.

When the tripe is ready, remove the pan from the heat and strain it, reserving the cooking liquid. Measure the liquid, and make it up to 550ml (1 pint) with more milk if necessary. Keep the tripe and onions warm whilst you make the sauce.

Melt the butter in a saucepan, stir in the flour and the mustard powder, and allow it to cook gently for 2-3 minutes, stirring, then gradually blend in the tripe cooking liquid, a little at a time, stirring constantly as you bring the sauce to the boil and it thickens. Reduce the heat and add the tripe and onions to the sauce, then simmer the mixture for 10 minutes, without allowing it to boil.

Turn out the tripe and onions into a warmed serving bowl and garnish with finely chopped fresh parsley. Serve immediately, piping hot, with potatoes and seasonal vegetables.

RETFORD, CANNON SQUARE 1954 R261028

NOTTINGHAMSHIRE PIE

October 2008 saw the arrival of a 'new' traditional dish for Nottinghamshire, when the 'Nottinghamshire Pie' was officially launched by award-winning local chef Mr Roy Wood (see www.roywoodchef.co.uk). Mr Wood felt it was a shame that Nottinghamshire did not have its own distinctive traditional dish when so much wonderful food is produced in the county, so he created his pie 'for the county of Nottinghamshire' in hopes that it will become a traditional favourite in years to come. The 4 key ingredients of his delicious Nottinghamshire Pie are beef, leeks, potatoes and Stilton cheese, which are all produced within the county. Here is a dish you can be proud to serve up as a true 'flavour of Nottinghamshire'!

NOTTINGHAMSHIRE PIE ZZZ05666

(Photograph reproduced by kind permission of Mr Roy Wood – www.roywoodchef.co.uk)

NOTTINGHAMSHIRE PIE

This recipe is reproduced here by kind permission of its creator Mr
Roy Wood (www.roywoodchef.co.uk). Serves 4

> 900g/2 lbs diced beef (chuck steak)
> 40g/1½ oz flour, lightly seasoned
> 90g/3oz butter
> 2 whole leeks, trimmed, washed and chopped
> 2 sprigs of thyme
> 1.2 litres/2 pints beef stock
> 1 tablespoon wholegrain mustard
> 900g/2 lbs potatoes, peeled, boiled, mashed and seasoned
>   (make this towards the end of the meat cooking time)
> 90g/3oz Stilton cheese (ideally, use a Stilton made in
>   Nottinghamshire - either Colston Bassett or Cropwell Bishop
>   - see page 6)
> 1 slice of bread, toasted, then grated to make breadcrumbs

Coat the meat with the seasoned flour. Put a large pan on the stove
to heat. Melt the butter in the pan then add the meat, and cook until
sealed on all sides. Add the leeks, mustard and thyme, and pour in the
stock. Simmer for 2 hours, stirring occasionally to ensure that it does
not stick to the bottom of the pan and burn.

Make the mashed potatoes whilst the meat is cooking.

Pre-heat the oven to 220°C/425°F/Gas 7. Check the meat is tender,
and the sauce is thickened, then pour it all into an ovenproof dish and
cover with the mashed potato. Top with the crumbled Stilton cheese
and then the breadcrumbs, then bake in the pre-heated oven for 20
minutes until the topping is golden brown. Serve piping hot with
steamed greens.

NB: Cooking times for the beef are dependent on the quality. Some
diced beef may take longer than the recommended time to tenderise.
Also, if your sauce does not look thick enough, either reduce it further
or thicken it with cornflour or granules.

ROBIN HOOD COUNTRY

For many people in Britain, Nottinghamshire is 'Robin Hood Country' – the place where the legendary folk hero Robin Hood and his band of outlaws, the 'Merry Men', lurked in Sherwood Forest, running rings around the hapless Sheriff of Nottingham. Sherwood Forest once covered over 100,000 acres between Nottingham and Worksop. As early as the 10th century, this vast tract of wooded landscape was known as 'sher wood', meaning 'the wood belonging to the county, or shire', and by the 12th century it was a royal forest subject to its own Forest Law. The view shown in photograph O131014 on page 27 is in the Sherwood Forest Country Park, an area of 450 acres with many of the best surviving ancient oak trees amid silver birch, younger oaks and bracken. Visitors may also catch glimpses there of fallow deer, and even roe and red deer.

It is not known for sure whether Robin Hood ever really existed – the Robin Hood of legend who stole from the rich and gave to the poor may be an amalgam of several historical figures – but in the later Middle Ages Nottinghamshire became the location for the stories about this much-loved outlaw that are still so popular today. Over the years various real places became connected with people in the tales, such as Sherwood Forest where the Merry Men lived, Edwinstowe where legend says that Robin married his true love Maid Marian, and, of course, Nottingham Castle, home of the evil Sheriff of Nottingham.

The names of Robin Hood and Nottingham have been inseparably linked for centuries, yet it was not until 1952, through the generosity of Nottingham businessman Philip Clay, that the city acquired a statue of one of its most famous characters, as seen in photograph N50090, opposite. It is positioned just outside the city walls.

NOTTINGHAM, THE STATUE OF ROBIN HOOD c1955 N50090

RECIPE

VENISON CASSEROLE

Robin Hood and his Merry Men had to poach their venison from Sherwood Forest at risk of their lives, but wild venison from the Forest is now available to anyone from good butchers in the area, and is also served in many local pubs and restaurants; you can also buy it in the form of venison burgers and sausages. Venison is a rich and well flavoured meat, low in cholesterol and high in iron. Nowadays it is also readily obtained throughout the country as farmed venison, which has helped revive its popularity. Venison can sometimes be dry, but a good way of cooking it is in a stew or casserole, as in this recipe, to make sure it is tender and juicy. It also makes a very good game pie in combination with other wild meat, such as wild boar – see the recipe on page 28.

> 1kg/2 lbs 4oz venison braising steak, cut into cubes
> 2 tablespoonfuls plain flour, seasoned
> 50g/2oz butter
> 2 tablespoonfuls oil
> 2 onions, peeled and thinly sliced
> 1 clove of garlic, peeled and finely chopped
> 600ml/1 pint stock
> 150ml/ ¼ pint red wine
> 1 tablespoonful tomato purée
> 225g/8oz carrots
> 115g/4oz mushrooms
> 2 dessertspoonfuls redcurrant jelly
> Salt and freshly ground black pepper

Pre-heat the oven to 180°C/350°F/Gas Mark 4. Toss the cubes of venison in the seasoned flour so that all sides are covered.

Melt half the butter and oil together in a flameproof casserole that
has a tight-fitting lid. Fry the venison, a few cubes at a time, until
all sides are browned. Put the browned meat to one side and keep
warm. Melt the remaining butter and oil in the casserole, add the
sliced onions and cook gently for about 10 minutes, until they are
soft and transparent, then add the finely chopped garlic. Stir in the
remaining seasoned flour and cook for 1-2 minutes, then add the
tomato purée, and then the stock and the red wine, a little at a time,
stirring continually. Increase the heat and bring the sauce to the boil,
constantly stirring as the sauce thickens. Season to taste with salt
and pepper, then add the sliced carrots and mushrooms and the
browned venison pieces. Put the lid on the casserole and cook in the
pre-heated oven for about 1½ - 2 hours. Stir the redcurrant jelly into
the casserole 10 minutes before serving. This casserole is even better
if it is made the day before needed, and reheated in the oven before
serving.

OLLERTON, SHERWOOD FOREST c1955 O131014

RECIPE

ROBIN HOOD PIE

This is another great recipe created for Nottinghamshire by the award-winning local chef Mr Roy Wood (www.roywoodchef.co.uk) and reproduced with his kind permission. Mr Wood devised this dish to celebrate the release of the feature film 'Robin Hood' in 2010, starring Russell Crowe and Cate Blanchett. It is a delicious pie with a bubble and squeak topping, filled with just the sort of wild game that Robin Hood and his Merry Men would have caught and eaten regularly in Sherwood Forest. Serves 6

For the pie filling:
900g/2 lbs diced game meat such as venison, wild boar and rabbit
2 tablespoonfuls of dripping
2 onions, peeled and sliced
2 carrots, peeled and sliced
120g/4oz diced pancetta
120g/4oz chestnut mushrooms, cleaned and halved
1 clove garlic, peeled and crushed
1 tablespoonful of redcurrant jelly
2 sprigs of thyme
30g/1oz plain flour
300ml/½ pint chicken stock
300ml/½ pint ale

For the bubble and squeak
900g/2 lbs mashed potato
1 onion, peeled and sliced
1 small cabbage, sliced and blanched
25g/1oz butter

Heat a thick bottomed pan, melt the dripping, then brown the pieces of game meat. Now stir in the onion, carrot, pancetta and mushrooms. Add the crushed garlic, redcurrant jelly and thyme, then mix in the flour and cook for a few minutes. Pour in the ale and stock and bring to the boil, then simmer for two hours or until the meat is tender.

Whilst the meat is cooking, make the bubble and squeak by frying the onion and cabbage in butter then mix in the mashed potato and cook until browned.

Pour the pie filling into a pie dish and top with the bubble and squeak. Cook in a hot oven (200°C/400°/Gas Mark 6) for 20 minutes. Serve with a chunky piece of fresh bread.

ROBIN HOOD AND MAID MARIAN FROM THE SHERWOOD FOREST VISITOR CENTRE TUCKING INTO A PORTION OF ROBIN HOOD PIE WHEN IT WAS LAUNCHED IN 2010 ZZZ05667
(Photograph reproduced by kind permission of Mr Roy Wood – www.roywoodchef.co.uk)

RECIPE

TOAD IN THE HOLE WITH NOTTINGHAMSHIRE SAUSAGES

Nottinghamshire sausages are available from several good butchers in the county. They are made with venison as well as pork, and are just the sort of meaty, well-flavoured sausages you need to use for this recipe.

> 450g/1 lb Nottinghamshire Sausages
> 175g/6oz plain flour
> A pinch of salt
> 2 eggs
> 600ml/1 pint milk and water mixed
> 15g/ ½ oz lard or dripping

Make the batter 1 hour before you start cooking the dish. Put the flour in a bowl with the salt, make a well in the centre and break in the eggs. Beat them into the flour, gradually adding the milk and water to make a smooth, creamy batter. Beat it well, then leave to stand for 1 hour. (This can also be prepared in a liquidizer.)

Pre-heat the oven to 220°C/425°F/Gas Mark 7. Melt the lard or dripping in a frying pan and brown the sausages nicely all over (this gives a better flavour than cooking the sausages in the oven). Pour the fat and sausages into a 30cm (12 inch) roasting tin. Place the tin in the oven for a few minutes to heat through, then remove from the oven, pour in the prepared batter and replace the tin in the oven. When the batter is nicely puffed up, reduce the oven temperature to 190°C/375°F/Gas Mark 5, and continue cooking until well-risen and golden brown – the total cooking time from start to finish should be 35-40 minutes.

WORKSOP, BRIDGE STREET c1965 W278025

NOTTINGHAM, THE MARKET SQUARE 1923 74594

NOTTINGHAM GOOSE FAIR

Nottingham's famous Goose Fair takes place in early October. It is a matter of conjecture how old the fair is, but tradition states that it dates from 1284, the year of the charter of Edward I. For many centuries geese were indeed the main commodity sold at the fair, as it coincided with the time when geese first became ready to eat, after fattening on the corn stubble after harvest time. In its heyday as a hiring fair and autumn market for the Midlands it is estimated that up to 20,000 geese changed hands at Nottingham Goose Fair each year. Huge flocks of geese would be driven on foot to Nottingham from Norfolk and Lincolnshire.

For many centuries Nottingham Goose Fair was held in the city's Market Square (seen as it looked in 1923 in the photograph on the previous pages). By the 18th century the emphasis of the fair had shifted from selling geese to selling cheese, enormous quantities of which were sold there each year, but geese continued to be sold in great numbers at Goose Fair time along the street in the city known as The Poultry. Originally intended as a market, during the 20th century Nottingham Goose Fair became a pleasure fair that is held for three days every October and is still a major event in Nottingham's year.

A favourite delicacy sold at Nottingham Goose Fair is a cup of mushy peas, made from dried marrowfat peas which are soaked in water overnight and then brought to the boil in a pot of water, and then slowly cooked at a gentle simmer, seasoned with a little sugar and salt, for a long time until they become soft - and mushy! It is a more skilful process than you might imagine to produce perfect mushy peas – get the balancing act wrong and you can end up with either a disappointing slop, or just a warm, wet pea without that magical mushy quality. Local people chomp their way through thousands of cups of mushy peas over the three days of Nottingham Goose Fair each year, seasoned the Nottinghamshire way with a dollop of mint sauce.

RECIPE

CHICKEN LEGS IN SPICY BARBECUE SAUCE

The recipe for the famous HP brown sauce was invented in the 19th century in Basford, in northern Nottingham, by shopkeeper Frederick Gibson Garton in his pickling factory behind 47 Sandon Street. It was popular with his customers but sadly Mr Garton failed to make his fortune with HP Sauce, as he sold the recipe and brand name for £150 to his vinegar supplier, Samson Moore of the Midland Vinegar Company near Birmingham, to settle a debt. Mr Moore launched HP Sauce commercially in 1903, to great success. Tradition says that Mr Garton told Mr Moore that he had named his sauce 'HP' as he had heard it was being served in a restaurant in the Houses of Parliament, but it has been suggested that he was joking and that 'HP' really stood for 'Home Produced'. This easy recipe may not be haute cuisine but it recalls the proud place of HP Sauce in Nottingham's culinary heritage by using it to make a spicy barbecue sauce that goes well with chicken, sausages and burgers. Any leftover sauce can be used cold, as a tasty relish. This amount serves 4-8 people, depending on appetite.

        50g/2oz butter
        1 medium onion, finely chopped
        1 clove of garlic, crushed or finely chopped
        1 x 400g (16oz) can of chopped tomatoes, and the juice
        2 tablespoonfuls of HP Sauce
        1 tablespoonful of runny honey
        Salt and pepper to taste
        8 chicken drumsticks
        Enough long-grain rice to serve 4 people

Combine the butter, chopped onions, garlic, tomatoes and their juice, HP Sauce, honey, and plenty of salt and pepper in a saucepan. Bring to the boil then reduce the heat to low, then gently simmer the sauce for about 30 minutes (uncovered) until it has thickened slightly, stirring occasionally to prevent it sticking to the bottom of the pan. Whilst the sauce is cooking, cook the rice and then keep it hot whilst you prepare the chicken drumsticks. Pre-heat the grill to hot. Place the chicken drumsticks in the grill pan and brush them liberally with the barbecue sauce. Grill the chicken drumsticks for 10 minutes on each side, brushing frequently with more sauce. Serve the chicken on a bed of cooked rice, with extra sauce spooned over them.

From the 18th century the great formal estates around Sherwood Forest which were owned by five dukes, including the Dukes of Newcastle and Portland, gave this area of Nottinghamshire its nickname of 'The Dukeries'. The five great ducal estates were Thoresby, Clumber, Rufford, Worksop Manor and the magnificent Welbeck Abbey near Worksop, which is shown in photograph W278044 (below). This vast and architecturally complex mansion, standing in its vast 3,000 acres grounds, is on the site of an abbey founded in 1153, of which fragments remain. After the Dissolution it eventually passed in 1597 to William Cavendish, grandson of the famous Bess of Hardwick, and then by marriage to the Dukes of Portland in 1734. Having for some years partly been occupied by an army college, it is now once again a private home. Housed in converted buildings in the grounds of Welbeck Abbey are The School of Artisan Food and the Welbeck Farm Shop, which sells Stichelton cheese made from the milk of a herd of cows on the Welbeck estate.

WORKSOP, WELBECK ABBEY c1955 W278044

RECIPE

WELBECK PUDDING

This unusual and delicious apple pudding is named after Welbeck Abbey, one of the stately homes of 'The Dukeries' in the north of the county (see opposite). It has a light, fluffy topping made of thickened milk and egg, rather like a soft meringue or a soufflé, although it does not contain flour.

> 2-3 tablespoonfuls apricot jam
> 675g/1½ lbs Bramley apples, peeled, cored and cut into slices
> 150ml/5 fl oz (¼ pint) milk
> 2 level dessertspoonfuls of cornflour
> 1 large egg
> 25g/1oz caster sugar

Pre-heat the oven to 180°C/350°F/Gas Mark 4.

Butter an ovenproof dish, about 900ml (1½ pint) capacity. Spread the apricot jam in a layer on the bottom of the dish. Fill the dish with the apple slices, spread evenly.

Blend the cornflour into a smooth paste in a pan with a little of the milk, then stir in the rest of the milk. Bring the milk to the boil over a medium heat, stirring constantly, until it has thickened. Remove the pan from the heat and leave the mixture to cool for a few minutes.

Separate the egg. Whisk the egg white as you would for a meringue, until it is stiff and fluffy and stands in soft peaks. Gently fold in the sugar. Beat the egg yolk with a fork then stir it into the thickened milk mixture, and mix well. Pour the whisked egg white into the pan, and carefully fold it into the mixture using a large metal spoon.

Pour the mixture over the apples in the dish, making sure that all the apple pieces are covered. Bake the pudding in the pre-heated oven for about 30 minutes, until the topping is risen and set, and light golden brown. Remove the dish from the oven and leave the pudding to cool for about 10 minutes, then serve warm.

RECIPE

MANSFIELD PUDDING

This hearty suet sponge pudding named after the Nottinghamshire town of Mansfield is flavoured with brandy and nutmeg. A recipe for Mansfield Pudding was included by Mrs Isabella Beeton in her famous 'Book of Household Management', first published between 1859 and 1861, and this is a modern adaptation of it. When this pudding comes out of the oven it is lovely and crisp on the outside, with a rich fruity filling.

50g/2oz fresh white breadcrumbs
300ml/ ½ pint milk
1 tablespoonful caster sugar
75g/3oz shredded suet
1 tablespoonful plain flour
115g/4oz currants
½ teaspoonful freshly grated nutmeg
2 eggs, beaten
1 tablespoonful of brandy
Extra caster sugar for serving

Pre-heat the oven to 180°C/350°F/Gas Mark 4.

Heat up the milk until it comes to the boil. Place the breadcrumbs in a large bowl, and pour over the hot milk. Leave to soak for 15 minutes, then stir in the sugar. Add the suet, flour, currants and grated nutmeg, then the beaten eggs, and the brandy. Stir thoroughly to combine the ingredients, then beat it all together well for 2-3 minutes.

Butter the inside of a 1.1 litre (2 pint) ovenproof dish or mould. Pour in the mixture, and bake in the pre-heated oven for 1-1¼ hours, until the filling is set and the top of the pudding is nicely browned and crisp.

Turn out the pudding onto a warmed serving dish, sprinkle with caster sugar and serve whilst it is hot and the outside is still crispy, with cream or custard.

MANSFIELD, MARKET PLACE 1951 M184027

An important occasion in Mansfield in the past was the July Fair, which celebrated the town being granted its Market Charter in 1227. A traditional dish that used to be made in Mansfield at the time of the fair was a gooseberry pie. For many years a highlight of the fair was the town's mayor cutting open a giant gooseberry pie in front of a large crowd in the market place, after which pieces of the pie were shared out amongst the onlookers. Smaller gooseberry pies were a speciality of Mansfield's butchers' and bakers' shops at fair time, made with a crisp hot-water-crust pastry like a pork pie; the pie was filled with gooseberries and brown sugar, and, after baking, a quantity of melted apple or redcurrant jelly was poured into the pie through a hole in its lid, and it was then left to cool. The resulting pie had a succulent fruit filling set in a fruity jelly, and was eaten cold. It was also a tradition in the past at the time of the fair to send gooseberry pies to Mansfield people living elsewhere in the country.

**NEWARK-ON-TRENT
CARTER GATE 1906** 56497

RECIPE

NEWARK PUDDING

A recipe for Newark Pudding was included in the Newark Cookery Book, published around 1890. This version is from an adaptation of that original recipe by Angela Geary in her book 'Our Local Food, Past and Present', published in 1994, which is full of traditional recipes and fascinating information about Nottinghamshire's food heritage.

1 pint of milk
25g/1oz fresh white breadcrumbs
2 eggs
1 tablespoonful of ground rice (you will find this
  near the pudding rice on supermarket shelves)
115g/4oz raisins
15g/½ oz butter
¼ teaspoonful bicarbonate of soda
1 tablespoonful caster sugar
½ teaspoonful vanilla essence

Pre-heat the oven to 180°C/350°F/Gas Mark 4, and butter an ovenproof dish of about 900ml (1½ pints) capacity. Put the breadcrumbs in a bowl, add half a pint of the milk and leave to soak for 5 minutes. Separate the eggs. Beat the eggs yolks well then stir them into the bread and milk, and mix it all together well to form a smooth mixture.

Melt the butter in a pan over a gentle heat. Mix the ground rice to a smooth paste with 2 tablespoonfuls of the remaining half pint of milk, and stir it into the bread mixture. Add the rest of the milk, the melted butter, raisins, sugar, vanilla essence and the bicarbonate of soda, and mix well. Whisk the eggs whites in a bowl as you would for a meringue, until they are stiff and stand in soft peaks, then gently fold the eggs whites into the mixture. Pour the mixture into the buttered dish and bake in the middle of the pre-heated oven for between 45 minutes and one hour – check it after 45 minutes and take it out if the top is browning too much, otherwise leave in the oven for a bit longer. The centre of the pudding should be lightly-set, soft and creamy, rather like the filling of a Bread and Butter Pudding. Serve from the dish, and hand round a little cream to pour over it.

BRAMLEY APPLES

Nottinghamshire has an honoured place in food history as the Bramley cooking apple originates from Southwell, a small minster town north-east of Nottingham. The first tree grew from an apple pip planted in a pot some time between 1809 and 1813 by Mary Ann Brailsford, a young girl who had taken some pips from apples her mother was cutting up for cooking; Mary Ann's apple seedling was then planted in her garden in Church Street, in the Easthorpe area of Southwell, and grew into a fine apple tree that bore excellent fruit. In 1846 the Brailsfords' cottage and garden was bought by Matthew Bramley, a Southwell butcher. Ten years later a local nurseryman called Henry Merryweather, impressed with the apples from the tree in Mr Bramley's garden, asked permission to take cuttings from it to propagate and produce the apple trees commercially at the Merryweather family's nursery in Halam Road in Southwell. Mr Bramley agreed on condition that the apple from the trees should be named after him. The site of the Merryweathers' nursery is now a housing development, but Mary Ann's original apple tree still stands in Southwell, in the garden of a house near the Bramley Apple pub in Church Street, and every Bramley apple tree in existence originates from it. Southwell commemorates its link with probably the finest cooking apple in the world with an annual Bramley Apple Festival and a delightful stained glass window in Southwell Minster, the Cathedral Church of Nottinghamshire.

SOUTHWELL, THE MINSTER, SOUTH EAST 1890 24089

RECIPE

BRAMLEY APPLE PIE

The Bramley apple which originates from Southwell in Nottinghamshire makes excellent purée, so is the apple of choice for stewing and making sauce to serve with pork, duck and goose. It is also ideal for baked apples, apple dumplings, crumbles and charlottes, but above all the Bramley is the finest apple for use in apple pies. As the novelist Jane Austen wrote in a letter to her sister in 1815, 'Good Apple Pies are a considerable part of our domestic happiness'.

<u>For the pastry:</u>
(Or use 225g/8oz ready-made sweet shortcrust pastry if preferred)
225g/8oz plain flour
50g/2oz butter
50g/2oz lard, refined vegetable fat or hard margarine
  for pastry-making
Pinch of salt
1 rounded dessertspoonful caster sugar
2-3 tablespoonfuls cold water

<u>For the filling:</u>
900g/2 lbs Bramley apples (unprepared weight)
115g/4oz white or soft brown sugar (or a little more, to taste)
50g/2oz plain flour (2 level tablespoonfuls)
Half a teaspoonful ground cinnamon
50g/2oz sultanas (optional)
Juice of half a lemon
25g/1oz butter, cut into pieces

<u>To finish:</u>
1 egg, beaten
A little extra caster sugar

First of all, make the pastry. Sift the flour and salt into a mixing bowl, and stir in the dessertspoonful of sugar. Cut the butter and fat or margarine into small pieces and rub it into the flour with your fingertips until the mixture resembles fine breadcrumbs. Use a round-

44

bladed knife to stir in just enough cold water to make a soft (but not wet) dough. Turn out the dough onto a lightly floured surface and knead it gently and briefly until it is smooth and elastic. Wrap the dough in cling film or in a plastic bag and leave it in the fridge to 'rest' for 30 minutes. When the pastry is ready to use, pre-heat the oven to 200°C/400°F/Gas Mark 6, and place a baking tray in the oven to heat up. Grease a pie tin or dish about 22-26 cms (9-10 inches) in diameter. Roll out two-thirds of the pastry on a lightly floured surface, and use it to line the pie tin or dish.

Peel, quarter and core the apples, and cut them into thin or chunky slices as you prefer. Mix the apple pieces in a large bowl with the sugar, sift in the flour and cinnamon and mix well until the apple pieces are well coated. Mix in the sultanas if using. Turn the mixture into the pie tin or dish, heaping it up in the middle to form a mound. Sprinkle the lemon juice all over the filling, and dot small pieces of butter on the top. Brush round the pastry edge with some of the beaten egg. Roll out the rest of the pastry and use it to make a lid for the pie, trimming the edge. Press all round the edge of the pie with your thumb to seal the pastry edges well together. Cut two small crosses in the pastry lid with a sharp knife to allow steam to escape during cooking. Brush the lid of the pie with beaten egg, and sprinkle a little caster sugar over it.

Place the pie on the baking tray in the pre-heated oven (this helps the pastry base of the pie to cook through). Cook for 15 minutes, then reduce the heat to 190°/375°/Gas Mark 5 and cook for a further 25-30 minutes, or until the pastry is crisp and golden. Remove from the oven and sprinkle some extra sugar over the top whilst the pie is still hot. Leave the pie to 'rest' for 10 minutes before serving.

BRAMLEY APPLES F6134

RECIPE

DAMSON AND APPLE TANSY

The Merryweather family's plant nursery at Southwell where the Bramley apple was first propagated and sold commercially was also where the Southwell Redcurrant and the Merryweather Damson were developed. The Merryweather Damson is now one of the most widely-grown of all damson varieties, producing good crops of large, well-flavoured fruit. This old English recipe using damsons took its name from the bitter-tasting herb of tansy that was used in the past for flavouring sweet dishes – however, 'tansy' is now used to describe a buttered fruit purée made with eggs and breadcrumbs, and the flavour is sharpened with lemon juice instead. If you can't find damsons to make this dish, try using plums instead.

225/8oz damsons, cut in half and de-stoned
225g/8oz Bramley cooking apples, peeled, cored and sliced
50g/2oz unsalted butter
115g/4oz caster sugar
2 egg yolks, beaten
4 level dessertspoonfuls of fresh white breadcrumbs
150ml/ ¼ pint double cream
1 dessertspoonful of lemon juice

Melt the butter in a heavy-bottomed saucepan with 70ml (2½ fl oz) of cold water, cover the pan with its lid and boil the fruit over a low heat until it is soft, stirring from time to time to prevent sticking and burning. Remove the pan from the heat and either push the fruit though a coarse sieve or put it through a blender, to form a purée. Return the purée to the pan and stir in the sugar – add a little extra to taste if necessary. If the purée seems rather thin, cook it over a low heat until it has reduced down and thickened to a dropping consistency. Remove the pan from the heat and allow the purée to cool a little, then mix in the beaten egg and the breadcrumbs. Return the pan to a low heat and cook, stirring continually, until the mixture has thickened, then leave to cool. Lightly whisk the cream and fold it into the cooled damson mixture. Add a little lemon juice to taste, to sharpen the flavour. Spoon the mixture into individual serving dishes or glasses and chill in the refrigerator for at least one hour before serving.

RECIPE

NOTTINGHAM PUDDING

This traditional pudding from Nottinghamshire, of Bramley apples baked in a batter blanket with a crisp top and a soft centre, is a filling dish ideal for a cold winter's day. It is also known as Apple-in-and-Out. This quantity is enough for 6 people.

6 even-sized Bramley cooking apples
75g/3oz butter
75g/3oz soft brown sugar
Half a teaspoonful ground nutmeg
1 teaspoonful ground cinnamon
175g/6oz plain flour
Water
3 eggs, beaten
Salt
450ml/ ¾ pint milk

Pre-heat the oven to 200°C/400°F/Gas Mark 6.

Peel and core the apples. Cream the butter and sugar, and add the nutmeg and cinnamon. Fill the centre of each apple with the mixture. Place the apples in a large well-buttered ovenproof dish – it should be a deep dish, with the top of the apples level with its rim, then the batter should rise up and cover the apples during the cooking process.

Blend the flour with a little cold water and add the well-beaten eggs to it with a pinch of salt and sufficient milk to make a thick creamy batter. Pour the batter over the apples and bake the pudding in the pre-heated oven for 40-50 minutes, until the apples are soft and the batter is risen, golden brown and crisp. Serve immediately, with cream or custard.

RECIPE

NOTTINGHAM GINGERBREAD

225g/8oz plain flour
4 level teaspoonfuls ground ginger
1 teaspoonful bicarbonate of soda
115g/4oz butter or margarine
115g/4oz soft brown sugar
115g/4oz golden syrup
115g/4oz black treacle
150ml/ ¼ pint milk
1 egg, beaten

Pre-heat the oven to 160°C/325°F/Gas Mark 3. Grease an 18-20cm (7-8 inch) square cake tin, and line the sides and bottom of the tin with greased greaseproof paper.

Sieve together into a bowl the flour, ground ginger and bicarbonate of soda. Place the butter or margarine, brown sugar, syrup, treacle and milk in a heavy-bottomed saucepan and melt it over a low heat, stirring continually. When everything has melted, remove the pan from the heat and allow the mixture to cool a little, then add the mixture to the dry ingredients, together with the beaten egg. Beat the mixture well for five minutes, until it is smooth and well combined. Pour the mixture into the prepared tin and level it evenly.

Cook in the pre-heated oven for about one hour, until the top is springy and the gingerbread is coming away from the sides of the tin. When cooked, turn out carefully onto a wire tray, remove the paper and allow the gingerbread to cool completely before cutting into squares, then store in an airtight container. This gingerbread should be stored for several days before eating, so that it becomes sticky.

NOTTINGHAM, WHEELER GATE 1902 48327

PINDER'S

PERSON
CA
SPIRIT

RECIPE

PIKELETS

Pikelets, or pyclets if you prefer, are popular all over the Midlands, but the argument over whether they are the same thing as crumpets, and whether or not they should be cooked in a metal ring to contain the batter, seems to be a question of your own family tradition. However, for many people crumpets are cooked with the batter contained in a special metal ring on the pan or griddle, and pikelets are cooked as spoonfuls of batter dropped on to the pan or griddle – thus pikelets are thinner than crumpets, and not cooked into an even round shape, as crumpets are. Whether you call them pikelets or crumpets, the top surface of these yeasted doughy delicacies becomes covered with holes during the cooking process. When you spread them with butter, hot from the pan, the melted butter oozes into the holes – perfect for winter teatimes! This recipe uses dried yeast, but if you can find fresh yeast, use 15g/ ½ oz and cream it with a little sugar and some of the warmed water, then leave in a warm place to activate and go frothy before using. This quantity makes about 12 pikelets.

450g/1 lb plain flour (strong white breadmaking flour is best)
350ml/12 fl oz milk, warmed
350ml/12 fl oz water, warmed
7g/ ¼ oz dried yeast (2 heaped teaspoonfuls)
2 level teaspoonfuls salt
1 teaspoonful caster sugar
1 level teaspoonful baking powder
A little sunflower or vegetable oil for greasing the pan or griddle

Place the flour, sugar and dried yeast into a bowl and make a well in the centre. Pour in the warmed water and milk (add the yeast mixture now, if using fresh yeast). Gradually stir the flour into the liquid until you have a creamy batter with no lumps, and beat it well. Cover the bowl with cling film and leave in a warm place for at least an hour until the batter has risen and is bubbly.

Lightly grease a frying pan or griddle (and crumpet rings if using), and place on a medium to high heat. Whisk the salt and the baking powder into the batter. When the pan is hot, drop a good tablespoonful of the mixture into the pan and cook for about five minutes, or if using crumpet rings, place a ring in the pan and drop in enough mixture to fill to just below the top. Lots of holes should form on the surface of the pikelet as it cooks – if not, the mixture is too thick, so whisk some more water into the batter mix before making more. Cook the pikelet on one side for about 5 minutes until the surface is just set, then flip it over (or take it out of the ring and turn it) and cook the other side for about 2 minutes, until it is golden. When each pikelet is cooked, remove it from the pan and keep warm whilst you cook the rest of the batter. Either eat at once whilst they are hot, spread with butter, or cool on a wire tray and keep for toasting later.

WORKSOP, THE PRIORY GATEHOUSE c1955 W27805I

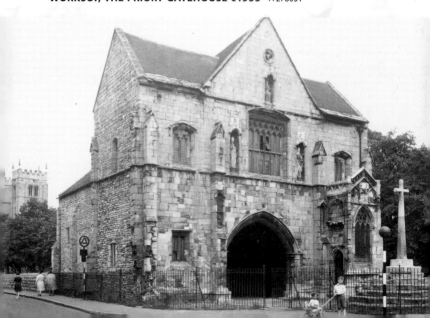

RECIPE

HAZELNUT BISCUITS

A cultivated variety of hazelnut ('Corylus avellana') is named after Nottingham and is commercially grown in the UK, the cultivar 'Nottingham Cobnut', also known as 'Pearson's Prolific'. Cobnuts are broader and longer than hazelnuts. Use Nottingham Cobnuts in this recipe if you can find them, but otherwise any hazelnut you can get will be fine. The nuts can be ground in a coffee grinder or zapped in a blender or liquidiser, but it is much easier to grind up chopped nuts rather than whole nuts. These sweet biscuits are lovely on their own, but also as an accompaniment to a creamy pudding or ice-cream. This quantity makes about 16 biscuits.

> 115g/4oz shelled hazelnuts, or chopped hazelnuts
> 150g/5oz plain flour
> A pinch of salt
> 115g/4oz butter, softened
> 50g/2oz caster sugar

If using whole nuts, spread them in a roasting tray and toast them in a moderate oven (190°C/375°F/Gas Mark 5) for 10 minutes, then rub off their skins. Grind the nuts to a powder in a coffee mill or blender. Don't worry if a few bits of nut remain in your 'nut flour' after grinding – this will add interest to the biscuits. Cream the softened butter and the sugar together, then add the flour, salt and ground nuts and mix it all together well (this can be done in a food mixer if preferred). Knead the dough lightly for a few minutes, then chill it in the fridge for 30 minutes. Pre-heat the oven to 190°C/375°F/Gas Mark 5. Grease a baking tray and line it with greaseproof paper. Roll out the dough on a lightly floured surface to about 1cm (half an inch) thick, and cut it into rounds about 5cm (2 inches) in diameter with a biscuit cutter. Place the biscuits on the prepared baking tray and bake in the pre-heated oven for 7-10 minutes, until they are golden but not too browned – it is important not to overcook them. Remove from the oven and leave to cool on the tray for five minutes to firm up slightly, then put them a wire tray to cool completely. Store in an airtight container.

RECIPE

STILTON AND WALNUT SCONES

Finally, a recipe for savoury scones using Nottinghamshire Stilton cheese. These are delicious warm from the oven, perhaps split in half and spread with butter, or with more cheese. They can be either served on their own as a savoury snack, or as an accompaniment to soup – why not serve them with the Leek and Potato Soup on page 2. They are also good eaten cold – try them split in half and spread with a herby cream cheese. This amount should make about 14 scones.

> 250g/9oz self-raising flour, plus a little extra to dust over the scones before baking
> 1 teaspoonful bicarbonate of soda
> ½ teaspoonful salt
> 50g/2oz butter or margarine, cut into small pieces
> About 175ml/6fl oz milk (or even better, buttermilk if you can find it – look for it by the cream in supermarkets)
> 150g/5oz Colston Bassett or Cropwell Bishop Stilton cheese, cut into small cubes about 1cm (½ inch) square
> 115g/4oz walnuts, roughly chopped

Pre-heat the oven to 200°F/400°F/Gas Mark 6. Grease two baking sheets. Sift the flour, bicarbonate of soda and salt into a large bowl. Add the diced butter or margarine, then rub it into the flour, using your fingertips, until the mixture resembles fine breadcrumbs. Stir in the cubed cheese and chopped walnuts, then mix in as much of the milk or buttermilk as necessary to form a soft but firm dough. Knead the dough very lightly for a minute or so, until it is smooth. Gently roll out the dough on a lightly floured surface to about 2.5cms (1 inch) thick. Use a biscuit cutter about 5-6cms (2 inches) in diameter to stamp out rounds of dough – do not twist the cutter as you press down, as this will affect the rising of the scone. Place the rounds on the greased baking sheets, lightly dust them with flour, and bake in the pre-heated oven for 15-20 minutes, until risen and golden brown. Leave the scones to rest on the baking sheets for two minutes, before carefully sliding them off onto a wire rack.

FRANCIS FRITH

PIONEER VICTORIAN PHOTOGRAPHER

Francis Frith, founder of the world-famous photographic archive, was a complex and multi-talented man. A devout Quaker and a highly successful Victorian businessman, he was philosophical by nature and pioneering in outlook. By 1855 he had already established a wholesale grocery business in Liverpool, and sold it for the astonishing sum of £200,000, which is the equivalent today of over £15,000,000. Now in his thirties, and captivated by the new science of photography, Frith set out on a series of pioneering journeys up the Nile and to the Near East.

INTRIGUE AND EXPLORATION

He was the first photographer to venture beyond the sixth cataract of the Nile. Africa was still the mysterious 'Dark Continent', and Stanley and Livingstone's historic meeting was a decade into the future. The conditions for picture taking confound belief. He laboured for hours in his wicker dark-room in the sweltering heat of the desert, while the volatile chemicals fizzed dangerously in their trays. Back in London he exhibited his photographs and was 'rapturously cheered' by members of the Royal Society. His reputation as a photographer was made overnight.

VENTURE OF A LIFE-TIME

By the 1870s the railways had threaded their way across the country, and Bank Holidays and half-day Saturdays had been made obligatory by Act of Parliament. All of a sudden the working man and his family were able to enjoy days out, take holidays, and see a little more of the world.

With typical business acumen, Francis Frith foresaw that these new tourists would enjoy having souvenirs to commemorate their days out. For the next thirty years he travelled the country by train and by pony and trap, producing fine photographs of seaside resorts and beauty spots that were keenly bought by millions of Victorians. These prints were painstakingly pasted into family albums and pored over during the dark nights of winter, rekindling precious memories of summer excursions. Frith's studio was soon supplying retail shops all over the country, and by 1890 F Frith & Co had become the greatest specialist photographic publishing company in the world, with over 2,000 sales outlets, and pioneered the picture postcard.

FRANCIS FRITH'S LEGACY

Francis Frith had died in 1898 at his villa in Cannes, his great project still growing. By 1970 the archive he created contained over a third of a million pictures showing 7,000 British towns and villages.

Frith's legacy to us today is of immense significance and value, for the magnificent archive of evocative photographs he created provides a unique record of change in the cities, towns and villages throughout Britain over a century and more. Frith and his fellow studio photographers revisited locations many times down the years to update their views, compiling for us an enthralling and colourful pageant of British life and character.

We are fortunate that Frith was dedicated to recording the minutiae of everyday life. For it is this sheer wealth of visual data, the painstaking chronicle of changes in dress, transport, street layouts, buildings, housing and landscape that captivates us so much today, offering us a powerful link with the past and with the lives of our ancestors.

Computers have now made it possible for Frith's many thousands of images to be accessed almost instantly. The archive offers every one of us an opportunity to examine the places where we and our families have lived and worked down the years. Its images, depicting our shared past, are now bringing pleasure and enlightenment to millions around the world a century and more after his death.

For further information visit: www.francisfrith.com

INTERIOR DECORATION

Frith's photographs can be seen framed and as giant wall murals in thousands of pubs, restaurants, hotels, banks, retail stores and other public buildings throughout Britain. These provide interesting and attractive décor, generating strong local interest and acting as a powerful reminder of gentler days in our increasingly busy and frenetic world.

FRITH PRODUCTS

All Frith photographs are available as prints and posters in a variety of different sizes and styles. In the UK we also offer a range of other gift and stationery products illustrated with Frith photographs, although many of these are not available for delivery outside the UK – see our web site for more information on the products available for delivery in your country.

THE INTERNET

Over 100,000 photographs of Britain can be viewed and purchased on the Frith web site. The web site also includes memories and reminiscences contributed by our customers, who have personal knowledge of localities and of the people and properties depicted in Frith photographs. If you wish to learn more about a specific town or village you may find these reminiscences fascinating to browse. Why not add your own comments if you think they would be of interest to others? See **www.francisfrith.com**

PLEASE HELP US BRING FRITH'S PHOTOGRAPHS TO LIFE

Our authors do their best to recount the history of the places they write about. They give insights into how particular towns and villages developed, they describe the architecture of streets and buildings, and they discuss the lives of famous people who lived there. But however knowledgeable our authors are, the story they tell is necessarily incomplete.

Frith's photographs are so much more than plain historical documents. They are living proofs of the flow of human life down the generations. They show real people at real moments in history; and each of those people is the son or daughter of someone, the brother or sister, aunt or uncle, grandfather or grandmother of someone else. All of them lived, worked and played in the streets depicted in Frith's photographs.

We would be grateful if you would give us your insights into the places shown in our photographs: the streets and buildings, the shops, businesses and industries. Post your memories of life in those streets on the Frith website: what it was like growing up there, who ran the local shop and what shopping was like years ago; if your workplace is shown tell us about your working day and what the building is used for now. Read other visitors' memories and reconnect with your shared local history and heritage. With your help more and more Frith photographs can be brought to life, and vital memories preserved for posterity, and for the benefit of historians in the future.

Wherever possible, we will try to include some of your comments in future editions of our books. Moreover, if you spot errors in dates, titles or other facts, please let us know, because our archive records are not always completely accurate—they rely on 140 years of human endeavour and hand-compiled records. You can email us using the contact form on the website.

Thank you!

For further information, trade, or author enquiries
please contact us at the address below:

**The Francis Frith Collection, Oakley Business Park,
Wylye Road, Dinton, Wiltshire SP3 5EU England.**
Tel: +44 (0)1722 716 376 Fax: +44 (0)1722 716 881
e-mail: sales@francisfrith.co.uk **www.francisfrith.com**